Tax Planning Review 1979

by
Leslie Livens ATII
Neil Thomas MA

Consultants
J. F. Avery Jones MA, LLB, FTII
Solicitor

E. E. Ray BCom, FCA, ATII
of Spicer and Pegler

LONDON
BUTTERWORTHS
1979

ENGLAND: Butterworth & Co. (Publishers) Ltd.
London: 88 Kingsway, WC2B 6AB

AUSTRALIA: Butterworths Pty. Ltd.
Sydney: 586 Pacific Highway, Chatswood, NSW 2067
Also at Melbourne, Brisbane, Adelaide and Perth

CANADA: Butterworth & Co. (Canada) Ltd.
Toronto: 2265 Midland Avenue, Scarborough M1P 4S1

NEW ZEALAND: Butterworths of New Zealand Ltd.
Wellington: 77-85 Customhouse Quay

SOUTH AFRICA: Butterworth & Co. (South Africa) (Pty.) Ltd.
Durban: 152/154 Gale Street

U.S.A.: Butterworth & Co. (Publishers) Inc.
Boston: 19 Cummings Park, Woburn, Mass. 01801

ISBN: 0 406 39675 2

Preface

This review brings together, under relevant headings, the vital tax developments of 1978, including all material available up to 1 January 1979.

It is designed to give all those working in taxation a reference point from which to take stock of the many changes that have occurred in the last twelve months, to assess their immediate implications for 1979, and then to plan accordingly.

The value of the work is in that—

- primarily, it identifies those vital tax developments that will create a tax planning requirement;
- secondly, it condenses that information to exclude the irrelevant and allow easy assimilation.
- thirdly, it arranges the developments in a logical and easily accessible form; and
- fourthly, it presents all this essential information conveniently and attractively.

It is our hope, therefore, that the book makes "order out of chaos" and contributes to efficient tax planning at all levels.

9 January 1979

L.L.
N.T.

Acknowledgements
We should like to acknowledge assistance from J. E. Redman LLB who contributed substantial material for the section on Capital Transfer Tax, and from C. A. Barcroft ATII, J. E. Newman MA, ACA, and Colin Davis MA, FCA.

Contents

Arranged in the same alphabetical order as in the book.

Capital Allowances

Agricultural buildings allowances: accelerated relief
                                             fish-rearing concession

Industrial buildings allowances: hotels
                                             long leases

Mining allowances
Patents allowances
Plant and machinery: car leasing
                          first year allowances
                          lessors and fire safety
                          nature of plant
                          provision of plant
                          renewals basis
                          sports grounds

Agricultural buildings allowances
FA 1978, s.39

Accelerated relief.   FA 1978 introduced an initial allowance of 20 per cent. (in addition to the existing 10 per cent. writing down allowance) into the scheme of agricultural buildings allowances.

Planning points.   The increased allowance is available to the person who incurs qualifying expenditure after 11 April 1978.

Taxpayers can choose whether or not to take full advantage of this initial allowance. A company can disclaim it wholly or in part, whilst an individual or partnership can specify the amount of it that is required. The company's disclaimer must be in writing within two years of the end of the accounting period in which the expenditure is incurred.

The maximum relief in the first year is 30 per cent. (up to 20 per cent. initial allowance plus 10 per cent. writing down allowance).

The permutations are endless within the existing 10-year period, and will need to be tied in with the new averaging provisions (see p.46), as well as existing reliefs such as stock relief (and clawback), personal relief, retirement annuity relief, etc.

Extended meaning of husbandry.   By extra-statutory concession B2, "husbandry" is now treated as including any method
of intensive rearing of fish on a commercial basis for the
production of food for human consumption.

This means that expenditure incurred in respect of fish farms is
now within the scope of agricultural buildings allowances and
claims should be considered. (See Simon's Tax Intelligence,
20 January 1978, p.27.)

Industrial buildings allowances: Hotels
FA 1978, s.38 and Sch.6

Outline.   Any capital expenditure, incurred after 11 April
1978 on the construction or extension of an hotel with at least
10 bedrooms, qualifies for capital allowances at the rate of 20
per cent. initial allowance and 4 per cent. annual allowance. A
size restriction is to ensure that only hotels which provide
minimum services and are large enough to make a worthwhile
contribution to the tourist industry qualify.

Provisions govern the extent to which an hotel qualifies for
these allowances, but a *de minimis* rule allows the full capital
expenditure to qualify, provided any non-qualifying part of
the total cost of construction does not exceed 10 per cent.

The costs of construction or extension of an hotel in the UK,
or elsewhere, qualify, provided that the trade of hoteliers is
carried on in that building and the profits are assessable to UK
tax. Reference is made to a 12-month period of use. The
allowances are available to freeholders, lessors or lessees (see
long leases, below) who incur expenditure on qualifying
hotels.

When trade ceases, the hotel is no longer a qualifying hotel.
Balancing adjustments are made according to the usual rules
on disposals of industrial buildings, but also two years after
the hotel ceases to be a qualifying hotel without being sold.
Temporary disuse, for example after a fire, is no bar to a hotel
remaining a qualifying hotel, but the disuse must not exceed
two years.

The purchaser of a qualifying hotel will be entitled to allowances even if the hotel is sold at a time when it is not a
qualifying hotel, provided it is reactivated as one.

Planning points. The basic test is that the hotel accommodation must be provided in a building or buildings of a permanent nature.

- "hotel" includes an inn, motel, holiday camp and a guest house, but nursing homes, Old People's homes and similar hostels are excluded.
- if accommodation is provided in separate buildings (for example chalet-style hotels), the expenditure on separate buildings would qualify, provided the separate buildings are within common curtilage. It seems likely that a separate building in which, say, only a swimming pool is housed, would not qualify.

Staff accommodation, even on a separate site, which is provided for, and in welfare use by, the hotel workers is included in a qualifying hotel: but this would not extend to flats or houses provided for individual workers. Worker occupied hostels are the intended objects of this widening of the relief.

In the case of an hotel carried on by an individual, whether alone or in partnership, accommodation normally used as a dwelling by that person, or by any member of his family or household, is excluded. This only applies during the "season". Such occupation by directors of companies would be subject to existing benefits legislation but for representative occupation of employees see FA 1977, s.33.

The "permanent nature" requirement excludes from relief movable accommodation such as caravans and tents but prefabricated structures might pass this test.

The other tests to be applied are—
The hotel must open for at least four months (120 days) in the "season", which means the seven months from 1 April to 31 October.
There was some concern about those hotels whose season was during the winter, but the Revenue maintain that they have no examples of hotels open in winter but not in summer.
When open in the season the hotel must have:

(*a*) at least 10 "letting bedrooms". (If an extension is built and as a result the hotel has 10 letting bedrooms, the cost of the extension qualifies. All proposed extension work should be considered in this light); and

(*b*) sleeping accommodation which consists wholly or mainly of "letting bedrooms".

A letting bedroom is defined as a private bedroom available for letting to the public generally and not normally in the same occupation for more than a month. Hotels that cater only for permanent residents would fail on this point. However, the normal practice, as in seaside hotels, of permanent guests in winter but holiday guests in summer means that such hotels are not barred because the "season" test is limited to summer months only. Therefore only a limited amount of juggling with guests is likely to be necessary to ensure qualification under this head.

Services provided must normally include the provision (and not mere availability) of breakfast and evening meal, the making of beds and the cleaning of rooms.

Interaction with other allowances—

It is estimated that between 30 and 40 per cent. of the cost of construction of a new hotel would qualify for plant and machinery allowance. All relevant expenditure should therefore be isolated so that the plant or machinery allowance is obtained on qualifying items (up to 100 per cent. first year allowance).

Fire safety expenditure, an important element in hotel costs, qualifies for plant and machinery allowances under FA 1975, s.15. Expenditure on thermal insulation qualifies for plant and machinery allowances under FA 1975, s.14.

As a rough guide, the building is the setting for the business, and plant and machinery is the apparatus used in it. For example, movable partitions can be considered plant on the basis of the decision in Jarrold v. John Good & Sons Ltd. C.A. [1963] 1 All E.R. 141. Central heating, sprinkler systems, air conditioning, electric fires, would be considered plant. However, suspended ceilings, double glazing, false floors, electrical fittings are not considered to be plant.

Industrial buildings allowances: long leases
FA 1978, s.37; CAA 1968 Ch.1 Pt.1

Government policy is for development land to be retained in public ownership. Local authorities build factories on land that they own either freehold or on very long leases. These "advance factories" are let to industrialists on long leases at premiums which are equivalent to the cost of construction. In these increasingly familiar circumstances the industrial user would have been denied industrial buildings allowances because, under the old rules, the local authority retained the "relevant interest", yet the local authority, being exempt from tax has no use for the allowance. This anomaly has been rectified by FA 1978, s.37 with benefits going beyond the letting of advance factories, applying to all long leases of industrial buildings.

The section provides that on a joint election by lessor and lessee, industrial buildings allowances will be available in respect of a premium paid for a long lease (at least 50 years) of an industrial building taking effect after 15 February 1978 (which includes an hotel after 11 April 1978).

The election must be made within two years after the date on which the lease takes effect.

The date the "lease takes effect" is the date on which the lease is granted or, where later, the beginning of the term for which it is granted. This interpretation is derived from the Law of Property Act 1925.

Pre-1978 expenditure. It has been suggested that because some taxpayers believed that the allowance for long leases would also cover pre-1978 expenditure, the relevant unexpired expenditure as at February 1978 should qualify. The Revenue have stated that where taxpayers had genuinely been misled, practical solutions had been found. It is not immediately obvious what this means but it could be a point worth following up where doubt exists about pressing a claim. Otherwise on grounds of fairness, relief is not to be given retrospectively to the purchaser of an advance factory who had knowingly entered into the transaction, since other industrialists have taken other steps to ensure their title to relief.

Any capital sum paid on the grant of a long lease of an industrial building qualifies subject to the usual industrial buildings rules and anti-avoidance restrictions.

The most likely cases are spec-built factories in, for example, new towns, which are leased, after 15 February 1978, from the local authority.

The legislation has wider application than appears at first sight, and is not limited to the letting of new buildings. The right to make an election by lessor and lessee applies whenever a long lease of an industrial building takes effect after the specified date.

The treatment applies to all expenditure relating to the building(s) or structure(s) which are the subject of the lease and which is in relation to the lessor's interest.

A long lease is one which exceeds 50 years according to the rules in TA 1970, s.84 but ignoring options for renewal.

Certain hotels (see above) are now deemed to be industrial buildings and these new long lease provisions apply to them.

The rules in CAA 1968 Chapter 1 apply, but FA 1968, s.11(3) under which the creation of a lease does not affect the continuance of a relevant interest is not applicable in these cases. The allowances are—

Initial allowance   50 per cent. (but for qualifying hotels, 20 per cent., see above).

Writing down allowance   4 per cent. per annum on a "straight line" basis.

Balancing allowances and charges as under existing rules.

If the building has previously qualified for allowances, only writing down allowances will be available to lessees, and for the lessor a balancing allowance or charge will arise.

Plant in buildings let on long leases: buildings let on long leases can have fixed plant such as heating and air conditioning. Strictly, the lessee would not have title to capital allowances on such plant. However, one assumes that the Revenue would allow plant and machinery allowances to the lessee based on a proportion of the premium paid for the lease which could be attributed to the fixed plant. It goes without saying that any disposal value would have to be brought into account on the happening of certain subsequent events. The advantage of being able to claim 100 per cent. first year allowance for the plant proportion of the premium should not be overlooked.

The new provision does not apply where lessor and lessee are connected persons within meaning of TA 1970, s.533 or where the sole or main benefit to the lessor appears to be the obtaining of a balancing allowance.

It appears that existing pre 15 February 1978 leases could be cancelled and renewed, since anti-avoidance measures are not aimed at that.

Mining allowances

SP 4/78, Simon's Tax Intelligence, 17 November 1978, p.533

The Board of Inland Revenue have agreed that expenditure incurred by mining companies on unsuccessful applications for planning permission to extract minerals will, subject to certain conditions, qualify for mining capital allowances under CAA 1968, s.62. This follows the decision in E.C.C. Quarries Ltd. v. Watkis Ch.D. [1977] S.T.C. 578 which established that such expenditure was of a capital nature. Expenditure on successful applications where the mineral source goes into production will continue to be relieved under CAA 1968, s.60.

Patents allowances
Simon's Tax Intelligence, 20 January 1978, p.26

Sale of invented patent to an associate. By extra-statutory concession B17, where an inventor sells the patent rights in his invention to a company which he controls, for a sum less than their open market value, the assessment on the seller is restricted to the actual sale price, provided that the purchasing company undertakes to restrict its capital allowance claim to that amount.

Plant and machinery

Car leasing. See page 44 for the effects on capital allowances of the Revenue's policy on car leases where the rental is calculated by reference to a residual value which is lower than the expected open market value of the car at the end of the lease, and the car is then sold at that price to a person connected with the lessee.

First year allowances. Where circumstances change (e.g. further personal reliefs become available) before the end of a year of assessment, revised claims for first year allowances will be allowed even though the assessment has become final. (See CCAB Press Release, 6 July 1978, reproduced in Simon's Tax Intelligence, 14 July 1978, p.321.)

Lessors and fire safety. Relief is given to lessors who make contributions towards their tenants' fire safety expenditure, provided the expenditure satisfies the conditions of FA 1974, s.17.

By a new extra-statutory concession B16, the relief is also allowed where the lessor incurs the expenditure himself, if similar expenditure by the tenant would have qualified for relief. (See Simon's Tax Intelligence, 20 January 1978, p.26.)

From 23 November 1978, the concession is extended to capital expenditure on fire safety measures in trade premises in Northern Ireland and concession B16 has been revised. (See Simon's Tax Intelligence, 1 December 1978, p.548.)

Nature of plant. The case of Benson v. Yard Arm Club Ltd. Ch.D. [1978] S.T.C. 408 has further demonstrated the application of the functional test of whether an object is plant. Capital allowances were claimed on a ship used as a floating restaurant and on its attendant barge. The claim failed.

The commercial utility of particular premises, here the amenity of the floating restaurant, does not convert them into plant. They still remain the setting and not the apparatus and capital allowances are not due.

Provision of plant.   Expenditure on the provision of plant. This does not include money spent (e.g. interest and commitment fees) on a loan which is to be used for the acquisition of plant.

The term "expenditure on the provision of plant" in FA 1971, s.41 is not, however, limited to the bare purchase price of the plant but includes items such as transport and installations expenditure, Ben-Odeco Ltd. v. Powlson H.L. [1978] S.T.C. 460, at 464 and 472.

Renewals basis—change to capital allowances basis.   On a change from renewals basis to capital allowance basis, taxpayers are, by extra-statutory concession B2, permitted to claim capital allowances provided that where they use more than one item of a class of machinery or plant, they change basis for all items in that class. (Simon's Tax Intelligence, 20 January 1978, p.27.)

Sports grounds, FA 1978, s.40.   Capital allowances have been available to a person who incurs capital expenditure for safety purposes on a sports stadium used by him for trading purposes, but only where the stadium had been designated as requiring a safety certificate.

FA 1978 removes this designation requirement and capital allowances are available for safety expenditure which is incurred on a voluntary basis by traders—the allowances are not available to lessors. The expenditure must nevertheless be certified by the appropriate local authority.

These provisions have retrospective effect back to 1 August 1975 (the date that the Safety and Sports Grounds Act 1975 was passed). Claims and disclaimers can be made up to 31 July 1979.

Capital Gains Tax

Absolute entitlement

Booth v. Ellard, Ch.D. [1978] S.T.C. 487

Where there is a plurality of beneficial owners, two requirements have to be satisfied for the beneficiaries to be absolutely entitled as against the trustees within FA 1965, s.22(5); their **interests must be concurrent and not successive and those** interests must be the same. In such circumstances a transfer to the trustees by a beneficiary is not a chargeable disposal for CGT.

Chattels

FA 1978, s.45

From 1978-79 onwards, the limit for exemption from capital gains tax for *disposals* of chattels is raised from £1,000 to £2,000.

Planning points. It is worth pointing out that FA 1965, s.30 (chattels) applies only to a limited number of assets—

    (*a*) Chattels which are wasting assets used in a business and on which capital allowances are claimable, and

    (*b*) Any chattels which are not wasting assets; these are usually "collectors'" pieces, e.g. jewellery, pictures, antiques, etc.

(Chattels which are wasting assets are of course exempt under FA 1968, Sch.12(1), except those in (*a*) above.)

Marginal relief.   Previously this restricted the *tax payable* on disposals over £1,000 to an amount not to exceed one-half of the difference between £1,000 and the proceeds from disposal. From 1977-78 onwards, to fit in with the new reliefs for small gains (see below), the marginal relief is to be calculated on a different basis: if disposals exceed £2,000 (but £1,000 for 1977-78 only) the *gain* will be reduced by so much of it as exceeds 5/3rds the difference between the disposal and £2,000 (£1,000 for 1977-78 only).

As before, but with increased amounts, if a chattel is sold for £2,000 or less (previously £1,000), any loss is computed as if it were sold for £2,000 (previously £1,000).

Sets of articles are treated as a single asset and disposals must be aggregated in applying the exemption.

Returns by individuals are not required where chattels are acquired for £2,000 or less. Auctioneers need not return details where disposals by clients of chattels are £2,000 or less.

Debt on a security

For the avoidance case of W. T. Ramsay Ltd. v. I.R. Comrs. see p.58.

Where a loan is no more than a simple unsecured loan, in that it has none of the characteristics which enable it to be dealt in and, if necessary, converted into shares or other securities, it is not a "debt on a security" within FA 1965, Sch.7, para.11(1), and a loss on its disposal does not qualify as an allowable loss, Aberdeen Construction Group Ltd. v. I.R. Comrs, H. L. [1978] S.T.C. 127, see also Expenditure allowable, below.

Disposal of assets

For the avoidance case of Burnam v. Hedges & Butler Ltd., involving the question of beneficial ownership and nominees, see p.57.

Expenditure allowable

The "wholly and exclusively" rule of FA 1965, Sch.6, para.4(1)(a) was interpreted in the avoidance case of Eilbeck v. Rawlings, see p.61.

Where it is a true construction of a contract, a waiver of a loan can form part of the consideration so that a sum is paid not only for the transfer of say shares but also for the waiver of the loan, Aberdeen Construction Group Ltd. v. I.R. Comrs, H. of L. [1978] S.T.C. 127 (see also Debt on a security, above).

Gifts of business assets

FA 1978, s.46 and Sch.8

This new relief reduces the CGT impact on the lifetime gift of a business. Such transfers are also encouraged by CTT reliefs, see page 28.

A form of roll-over relief has been introduced where, after 11 April 1978, gains rise on gifts or disposals not at arm's length, of business assets used in the donor's business or of shares in the donor's family trading company. On a claim by donor and donee, the gain is rolled over, i.e. the acquisition value of the gifted asset is reduced by the gain that would have been chargeable.

The disposal must be by an individual (including a partner in a trading or professional firm) and the recipient must be a person (including a company, a trustee, or an individual) resident or ordinarily resident in the UK. Deemed disposals by trustees by absolute entitlement or termination of life interest are qualifying disposals for the relief. The relief also applies to the occupation of woodlands managed on a commercial basis and with a view to profits.

For individuals, business assets means those used by the individual in his trade, profession or vocation or in his family trading company and includes shares in such a company. For trustees, business assets means those used in a trade carried on by the trustees or, for deemed disposals, by the beneficiary who has an interest in possession (for a beneficiary becoming absolutely entitled) or by the beneficiary whose life interest terminates, and shares in a trading company where the trustees hold at least 25 per cent. of the voting rights. Any shares held by the beneficiary personally are not taken into account.

Agricultural property which is not a trading asset of the donor at the time of its disposal by gift, etc., but which qualifies for a CTT reduction under FA 1975, Sch.8 qualifies as a business asset. It should be noted that this new relief supersedes, from 11 April 1978, the existing relief afforded to gifts of agricultural property under F (No. 2) A 1975, s.55. Family company and trading company are as defined in FA 1965, s.34, but the revision to the shareholdings test for family companies by FA 1978, s.48 should be noted (see Retirement relief).

Retirement relief is given in priority to this new relief. (For the interaction, see Retirement relief.)

Where the asset has not been used wholly for the trade, the held-over gain is to be reduced by multiplying it by the fraction—

$$\frac{\text{period in which asset used for trade (in days)}}{\text{whole period of ownership (in days)}}$$

If the asset not wholly used is a building, the held-over gain is reduced to the part used for the trade.

In the case of gifts of shares in a family company which owns assets which are not business assets, e.g., investments or shares in subsidiaries, the held-over gain is reduced by multiplying it by the fraction—

$$\frac{\text{market value of the company's chargeable business assets}}{\text{market value of whole of the company's chargeable assets}}$$

This fraction is explained in Retirement relief.

If any consideration passes between donor and donee, the held-over gain will be the amount by which the market value of the business asset at the time of disposal exceeds the consideration given by the donee.

Loans and guarantees to traders—losses relief
FA 1978, s.49

This new capital gains tax relief applies to loans or guarantees given after 11 April 1978. Thus it is unlikely that the relief will be invoked for the next year or so until these recent loans go bad or recent guarantees are called up.

Losses on loans made after 11 April 1978 to a trader will be allowable for CGT purposes. Payments under guarantee will also be allowable where the guarantee is given after 11 April 1978.

The relief applies where trades, professions or vocations are carried on but not where the trade is one of lending money.

There are conditions as to loans which qualify not only for losses on loans but also in respect of payments under guarantees on loans—

(*a*) the money lent must be used by the borrower wholly for the purposes of a trade, etc., carried on by the borrower, including for the setting up of a trade, etc. Where part of a loan has been so used, that part might presumably qualify. However, it may not always be possible to fix how the loan is to be used and hindsight will need to be used when loans go bad.

(*b*) the borrower must be resident in the UK but the legislation leaves it open that residence can be either when the loan is made or when a claim is made that it is irrecoverable.

(*c*) loans between spouses (or those who become man and wife) and loans between members of the same group of companies (or between companies which become members of the same group) do not qualify. Where the loan comes from outside the group but is handed on from one member to another then if the loan is used for trading purposes throughout the loan only qualifies if it goes bad in the hands of the first borrower.

(*d*) the lender must not have assigned his right to recover the loan.

(*e*) for losses on loans, the loan must not be a debt on a security (which is a chargeable asset anyway) but guarantee payments on loans which are a debt on security qualify.

(*f*) the principal (not the interest) of the loan must be irrecoverable but there is no relief where the amount has become irrecoverable because of the terms of the loan or because of any act of omission by lender or guarantor. The loan must be demonstrated to be bad and not merely engineered to be so by any artificial means.

(*g*) for guarantee payments the loan must be clearly irrecoverable by the lender and the guarantor must not have assigned any rights to recovery. The spouse and group limitations apply to guarantor and borrower, and guarantor and lender respectively.

Any subsequent recovery will be treated as a capital gain of the person to whom the loss was deemed to have accrued. Recovery will include money or money's worth or the market valuation of assignments if not at arm's length.

Excluded from the scope of this relief are any amounts taken into account for income tax or corporation tax.

Part disposals of land
FA 1969, Sch.19, para.10 amended by FA 1978, s.51

If there is a part disposal of land and the consideration does not exceed £10,000, the consideration is deducted from the cost. This applies to any disposal after 5 April 1978. Previously the figure was £2,500.

Power of appointment over settled property
S/P 7/78, see Simon's Tax Intelligence, 24 November 1978, p.541

Following the cases of Hart v. Briscoe and Hoare Trustees v. Gardner [1978] S.T.C. 89, the Revenue will continue to take the view that where a power of advancement or a general power of appointment is exercised irrevocably, the assets to which it applies will normally pass into a new settlement; a charge on a deemed disposal by the trustees of the original settlement will arise under FA 1965, s.25(3).

The Revenue will take the view that where a special power of appointment is exercised, the assets to which the appointment applies will, in normal cases, remain subject to the original settlement as modified by the appointment, so that a deemed disposal for the purposes of FA 1965, s.25(3) does not result.

Private residences
FA 1965, s.29 amended by FA 1978, s.50

The owner-occupier exemption from capital gains tax is given to an employee who lives in job-related accommodation (defined at FA 1974, Sch.1, para.4A) and disposes of a residence which he *intends* (i.e. it does not matter if he does not actually do so) in due course to occupy as his only or main residence. This provision applies to periods of ownership after 31 July 1978.

Retirement relief
FA 1965, s.33 amended by FA 1978, s.48

Increase in amount of retirement relief.   For disposals by way of sale or gift of the whole or part of a business after 11 April 1978 by an individual who is aged 60 or more, the amount of capital gains tax exemption afforded as retirement relief is increased. For each year by which the individual's age exceeds

60, the new limit will be £10,000 (with a corresponding part for a part of year), rising to maximum relief of £50,000 at age 65. Previously, the levels were £4,000 and £20,000 respectively.

Period of ownership.   Whereas previously to qualify for the relief it was necessary to have owned a business, or the company was a family trading company and the shareholder a full-time working director, for 10 years, this period has now been reduced to one year. The amount of relief depends, from 11 April 1978, on both the age of the individual and the number of years of ownership which satisfy the conditions for relief. For one year's ownership the relief is 10 per cent. rising to 100 per cent. for ten year's ownership of the business or shares but dependent on the individual's age.

To find the amount of relief due, *multiply* the length of the period of ownership, *by* the age above 60, *by* £1,000.

The business can be successively owned by an individual, a partnership, and a company or in any other sequence.

By concession (D8), as amended by an Inland Revenue Press Release, 13 March 1978 (see Simon's Tax Intelligence, 24 March 1978, p.140), separate businesses, including those held through family companies of which the individual was a full-time working director, owned during the 10-year period, will be treated as the same business for the purpose of the relief.

It is understood that a short break in trading (i.e. no more than two years), will not bar entitlement to the relief although obviously the years of break(s) will not themselves be included in the maximum 10-year sliding scale of relief.

Family trading companies.   For disposals after 11 April 1978, the formula for the proportion of the gain to be exempted becomes—

$$\frac{\text{gain}}{\text{on}} \times \frac{\text{market value of company's chargeable business assets}}{\text{market value of all company's chargeable assets}}$$

Chargeable business assets means all assets used for the business except those on a disposal of which no chargeable gains would accrue. Goodwill and leasehold or freehold property, for example, are chargeable business assets but shares in a subsidiary are not. Chargeable assets means all assets except those on a disposal of which no chargeable gain, which in practice the Revenue interpret as meaning "no chargeable gain or allowable loss", would accrue. Chargeable assets and chargeable business assets would exclude cash, stock, debtors and in many cases plant. The previous formula was–

$$\frac{\text{gain}}{\text{on}} \times \frac{\text{market value of company's chargeable business assets}}{\text{market value of company's assets}}$$

The change means that the relief is denied to gains that can be attributed to the sale of chargeable assets held as investments by the family company. This same revised formula is used for the new Gifts of business assets relief.

The definition of a family company is amended to lower the minimum shareholding requirement to the individual owning or, in the case of a trustee, exercising at least 25 per cent. of the voting rights or, if he and his family together hold 51 per cent. of those rights, he holds at least 5 per cent. Previously the levels were 25 per cent., 75 per cent. and 10 per cent. respectively.

This revised definition is used for the new Gifts of business assets relief and for Roll-over relief.

For intended gifts, it must be noted that retirement relief is given in priority to the new gifts relief (see below). It will be important to ensure that the timing of disposals is right so that the maximum retirement relief is obtained by the donor with the remainder of the gift receiving the new gifts roll-over relief. This is because the greater the retirement relief, the smaller the held-over gain. This would benefit the donee on his ultimate disposals. Retirement relief is an effective CGT exemption whilst the new gifts relief is only a deferral of liability.

Right to annual payments due under deeds of covenant

Rank Xerox Ltd. v. Lane C. A. [1978] S.T.C. 449

No chargeable gain accrues on the disposal of a right to receive annual payments due under a covenant by virtue of FA 1965, Sch.7, para.12(*c*). It is immaterial that valuable consideration is given for the promise to make payments.

Rights under service agreement

O'Brien v. Benson's Hosiery (Holdings) Ltd. C.A. [1978] S.T.C. 549

A right to personal services under a contract of service, not being assignable, cannot have a market value and is not an asset under FA 1965, s.22(1). A sum received for the release of an employee from his service agreement is not chargeable to CGT.

Roll-over relief
FA 1978, s.33 amended by FA 1978, s.47

Roll-over relief on the replacement of business assets is extended in two directions where new assets are acquired after 11 April 1978. Computations on disposals in earlier years may thus be affected.

More than one trade carried on. Previously, the relief for more than one trade (except for groups of companies) was restricted to traders concerned with goods or services of the same kind. Now, where assets are sold in one trade and new assets acquired in another, both or all trades will be regarded as a single trade.

Individual shareholder of a family trading company. The relief is now available to an individual who is a shareholder of a family trading company where that individual owns and replaces an asset used in a trade carried on by that company, provided that the company qualifies as his family company at the time of both acquisition and disposal of the asset. "Family company" is defined in FA 1965, s.34 as amended by FA 1978, s.48 (see Retirement relief). However, the individual cannot roll over his gain against an acquisition by the company.

Groups of companies. For the Revenue view of roll-over relief for companies within a group, see p.35.

Sale of land

For the cases of Smart v. Lowndes and Simmons v. I.R. Comrs. on whether proceeds from the sale of land are capital or trading receipts, see p.51.

Small gains
FA 1978, ss.17, 44 and Sch.7

Outline. From 6 April 1977 small *gains* are to be exempt from capital gains tax and not small *disposals* as previously. The alternative charge is replaced by marginal relief but for 1977-78 only, the alternative charge basis may be used where this is to the taxpayer's advantage The charge to tax for individuals (and personal representatives of deceased individuals for the year of death and the two following tax years) will be as follows:

Net gains	*Charge to tax*
£1,000 or less	Nil
£1,000 to £5,000	15% of excess over £1,000
£5,000 to £9,500	£600 + ½ excess over £5,000
£9,500 +	30% of total gains

For *trustees,* the above basis of charge applies to trusts set up for the mentally disabled or those in receipt of attendance allowances, but for other trustees the charge to tax is as follows:

Net gains	*Charge to tax*
£500 or less	Nil
£500 to £1,250	50% of excess over £500
£1,250 +	30% of total gains

For *unit and investment trusts* the rate of tax is effectively 10 per cent. from 1 April 1977. The rate of credit on gains or disposals remains 17 per cent. up to and including 1979-80 but will become 10 per cent. from 1979-80 onwards.

This new relief does not apply to *companies* and the rate of corporation tax on capital gains remains effectively at 30 per cent.

Planning points.   Returns need not be submitted, unless an inspector so requires, where disposals do not exceed £5,000 and the gains do not exceed £1,000. But clearly net gains will need to be computed to test what exemption there is or what needs to be done to obtain maximum benefit from the new reliefs.

There will be no charge even if *disposal* proceeds are large, provided *gains* are small. In some circumstances, therefore, more valuable property could be given away where gains are small, with little or no capital gains liability, but of course CTT consequences will need to be considered.

Gains are computed in the normal way with losses deducted only so much as necessary to reduce the *gains* to £1,000. Losses of the year are deducted before losses brought forward or back from the year of death.

The above amounts apply to the aggregate gains of husbands and wives. Therefore, the levels of £1,000, £5,000 and £600 are apportioned between them in proportion to their gains less losses of the year. If only one of them has chargeable gains (for the year), he or she will receive the full relief.

Although unused losses are available to be carried forward,

any unused relief is not available for carry forward and will be lost if not fully utilised.

These reliefs may effectively be utilised by, amongst others, those going abroad who will cease to be resident and ordinarily resident, those retiring (see also retirement and gifts of business assets below), those making liquidations in family or small companies (so that shareholders can use the reliefs) and those contemplating gifts of assets.

Transfer of property—retention of life interest

For the avoidance case of Berry v. Warnett, see p.63.

Variations of dispositions taking effect on death
FA 1965, s.24(11) as substituted by FA 1978, s.52

The new CTT provisions (see p.30) regarding deeds of family arrangement and disclaimers made after 10 April 1978 apply to the capital gains tax legislation with effect from 31 July 1978. But it has been stated in Parliament that the new capital gains tax provisions will be administered from 11 April 1978.

The new rules are wider in their practical scope. They apply where the variation benefits persons outside the family and outside the class of original beneficiaries in the will. They also apply where the original beneficiaries had taken a benefit before carrying out the variation.

It is now provided that where, within two years of the death, any of the dispositions of the deceased, whether by will, intestacy or otherwise, are varied or disclaimed by an instrument in writing effected by the original beneficiaries, such variation or disclaimer does not constitute a disposal for capital gains tax purposes. On the contrary, the alteration is to be treated as having been made by the deceased and any disclaimed benefit as never having been given. The alteration takes effect for capital gains tax purposes, however, only if the parties give written notice that they so elect to the Board within six months of the alteration or such longer time as the Board allow.

The rule that the alteration takes effect from the death does not apply where it was carried out for consideration in money or money's worth.

The new provisions apply whether or not the estate has been administered.

Capital Transfer Tax

Planning points.   In CTT planning, it is vital to consider not only the CTT cost, but also the effect of *other* taxes (notably capital gains tax and stamp duty) on a transaction, and to compare those results with what the tax bill would be on death if nothing was done. In this exercise it has always to be borne in mind that, perversely, CTT reliefs and exemptions do not march in step with the CGT provisions.

Since, unlike estate duty, CTT is a *current* tax, a positive attitude is called for in the taxpayer, because lost opportunities may not recur. For instance, taking a simple small matter, the failure to make use in any one year of the annual £2,000 exemption may, in an estate of say £70,000 to £90,000, be equivalent to a deferred payment of £800 to the Inland Revenue. This loss to the beneficiaries is multiplied when the failure persists over a number of years or where the estate is larger.

Anti-avoidance
FA 1978, ss.69-72

Charge on termination of discretionary trust.   The previous rules allowed a person such as an open company to become absolutely entitled to assets of a discretionary trust without a CTT charge. The new provisions seek to remedy this unintended situation as from 11 April 1978, by treating transfers to a company on the termination of a discretionary trust, when no interest in possession subsists, as a capital distribution and therefore liable to tax (FA 1978, s.70).

Government securities in foreign ownership. Two avenues, for the avoidance of CTT by exploiting the exemption for government securities in foreign ownership (the gilts exemption), have been closed with effect from 20 April 1978.

Now, it is not possible to advance property from one discretionary trust to another without a charge to CTT unless the domicile and ordinary residence conditions of the beneficiaries are satisfied in both settlements. This prevents the practice whereby property was advanced from a settlement, with only UK beneficiaries, to a second settlement, which had only non-domiciled, non-ordinarily resident beneficiaries who could take advantage of the gilts exemption.

A further way of exploiting the gilts exemption was to arrange for a close company incorporated abroad and resident outside the UK to hold an interest in possession in settled property. Although it was possible to "look through" a close company with an interest in possession to treat the participators as entitled to that interest, if the settled property consisted of gilts, the company's interest would be excluded property and therefore free of CTT. This loophole is now closed and the look-through provisions apply also for the purpose of the gilts exemption. The exemption is therefore available only if the participators are all domiciled and ordinarily resident outside the United Kingdom.

These provisions also apply to determine whether all beneficiaries of a discretionary trust qualify for the gilts exemption where a company is a beneficiary (FA 1978, s.72).

Protective trusts. If a beneficiary under a protective trust forfeits his interest in possession he is now to be treated as remaining entitled to it. There is the drawback that the value of the settled property continues to be included in the beneficiary's estate, but on the other hand, the estate duty surviving spouse exemption will continue to apply after forfeiture. This provision came into operation on 11 April 1978, but only in relation to the forfeiture of an interest occurring after that date (FA 1978, s.71).

Sales of interests under settlements. These provisions remove the CTT exemption where settled assets revert to the settler or his spouse, or pass to charities, etc., in those cases where the recipient has purchased the reversionary (or other relevant) interest in the settlement. There is also withdrawal of transitional CTT relief where a UK domiciled beneficiary has purchased his interest from a person domiciled abroad, who would not himself be entitled to relief (FA 1978, s.69).

Business property relief

FA 1978, s.64

As part of the package of measures to help small firms, further relief has been given to business property. For transfers of controlling shareholders or interests in a business which are made after 26 October 1977, an increased relief of 50 per cent. applies. Transfers of assets which are used in a business, but owned by a partner or controlling shareholder, are still eligible for relief at the old 30 per cent. rate.

A new 20 per cent. business relief is introduced for transfer, after 26 October 1977, of unquoted securities owned by the transferor continuously for two years before the transfer, but which did not give him control of the company before the transfer. The two-year ownership requirement is satisfied if, under the capital gains tax provisions regarding company amalgamations, etc., the shares held are identified with other shares acquired at least two years earlier, which themselves would have qualified. Shares falling to be valued as related property, e.g. shares held by the transferor's spouse, are normally included in determining whether the transferor had control. However, the 50 per cent. relief is not to apply on a death where the related property valuation is displaced following a subsequent sale of the shares for less than their "related property" value, if the shares did not by themselves give control. In this case, the 20 per cent. relief will now apply.

A technical amendment is made to permit business relief to be available for amounts treated as capital distributions from a discretionary settlement. This has effect from 29 July 1976 when business relief was introduced.

Planning points—business relief and control definition. The new basis of relief, coupled with the change of definition of control (see below), gives rise to important changes in CTT planning. A number of calculations by reference to alternative proposals and to the likely valuation of the shares (or the interest in the business) will be necessary in order to seek the most advantageous way of making gifts. The following are the sort of questions which may present themselves.

In the case of a controlling shareholder, should he give away the majority of his shares in one fell swoop, getting the benefit of the 50 per cent. relief? If not, to what extent and in what order should gifts be made? Should he, if he wishes to be moderately generous only, give away only so much as will leave him with a control holding still, so that future transfers may also get relief?

If the related property rules apply, say in the case of a husband and wife who together have a control holding, which spouse in all the circumstances should give away shares? Here the question of the extent of the diminution in the estates of the spouses in coming down below the control barrier still needs consideration. It will usually still be better for the spouse with least shares to give away his or her holding and thereby bring the other's holding below the control barrier. But the latter's loss of the future 50 per cent. CTT relief will need to be taken into account, since a 51 per cent. holding with 50 per cent. relief may well produce a lower valuation for CTT than a large minority holding with only 20 per cent. relief.

All in all, the arithmetic on a number of different hypotheses is vital before taking action. Again, CGT as well as any possible agricultural reliefs also need to be considered. Having regard to the new definition of control, it will be necessary to review any cases of companies where "control on a particular question" at present resides with more than one shareholder, in order that 50 per cent. relief is not lost.

Control of a company
FA 1978, s.66

Control of a company is now restricted to voting control on all questions affecting the company as a whole. It is no longer possible for control to be attributed on the basis of voting power on any particular question. However, in determining whether a person has control, the voting power of certain classes of share is ignored. These are shares with voting power on the question of winding up the company (e.g. the rights of minority shareholders in certain circumstances), and/or on questions primarily affecting the class of shares concerned. This more severe definition applies to transfers made after 19 April 1978.

Discretionary trusts—failure to exercise rights
FA 1978, s.74

Failure to exercise a right is treated as a disposition only if the value of another person's estate is increased. Therefore, the failure to exercise a right which increased the value of property held on a discretionary or accumulation and maintenance trust did not give rise to CTT. This defect is rectified in relation to deemed dispositions after 10 April 1978. CTT liability now arises on an omission to exercise a right if, as a result of the omission, the value of the property subject to a discretionary or accumulation and maintenance trust is increased.

Dispositions within two years of death
FA 1978, s.68

The Revenue had adopted a position on the basis of the previous provisions that they did not cover either the situation where a beneficiary redirected assets he had already accepted, or the situation where the new recipient was outside the family or outside the beneficiaries named in the will. Both these propositions have been contested by the taxpayers on the basis of the old law. However, the new provisions, applying to instruments in writing made after 10 April 1978, put matters beyond doubt by allowing relief from CTT (as also CGT) in both these circumstances. Although the possibility of re-dividing the estate within two years of the death provides a most useful long-stop, it has to be borne in mind that any deed of variation will be subject to the normal charge of stamp duty, and does not preclude charges to income tax.

It also applies to other types of property, e.g. joint property, unexercised general powers of appointment and property the distribution of which is laid down by law, such as foreign rights of inheritance. However, it does not apply to excluded property and property in which the deceased has an interest in possession which accordingly cannot be varied under this provision.

Employee trusts
FA 1978, s.67

It is easier (or slightly less difficult), as from 11 April 1978, to make transfers of shares to an employees' trust free of CTT (and CGT). The transferor can keep some shares and the transfer will be exempt if on the transfer, or within one year, the trustees have more than half of the ordinary shares and voting control on all matters affecting the company.

Interest in possession
Pearson and others v. I. R. Comrs. Ch.D. [1978] S.T.C. 627

In the first CTT case, it was decided that the interest of a person who, under a settlement, was immediately entitled to the income from the settled property subject only to a power of the trustees to accumulate, was nevertheless an interest in possession, since it involved a present right to whatever income there was which had not been accumulated.

Life policies and deferred annuity contracts
FA 1978, s.73

This provision amends, with effect from 11 April 1978, the rule for the valuation of life policies and deferred annuity contracts for CTT purposes. It prevents the avoidance of CTT by the use of associated endowment and term life policies whereby, although the main part of the premium was allocated to the endowment policy, the real value attached to the term policy, written for the benefit of a third party.

Rates of tax
FA 1978, s.62 and Sch.10

These provisions give effect to the proposals for reducing the burden of CTT announced by the Chancellor in his mini-budget of October 1977. The threshold for each CTT band is increased by £10,000 for chargeable transfers after 26 October 1977. There is now a nil rate band up to £25,000 (in place of the previous £15,000), which is a useful margin for planning but which, once used, has gone. Where the individual has made transfers previously which exceed £15,000, he does not now pay any more CTT until he reaches £25,000. Where CTT is payable on an event after 26 October 1977, in respect of an earlier transfer (which could be additional CTT on a death within three years, deferred CTT on a sale of timber, or CTT on a work of art when the conditional exemption ceases) the tax is calculated on the new scale. In the case of mutual transfers, any grossing-up for a pre-27 October 1977 gift is on the old scale, so that the donor will not obtain full repayment.

Transfers to non-domiciled spouses
FA 1978, s.63

The cumulative limit for exemption goes up from £15,000 to £25,000 with effect from 27 October 1977. It appears that even if the £15,000 limit was exceeded before 27 October 1977, a further £10,000 may be transferred free of CTT.

Woodlands
FA 1978, s.65

Where an election has been made to defer CTT on woodlands included in an estate on death, a CTT charge arises when the timber is disposed of by reference to the disposal proceeds. Any such disposal after 26 October 1977, will attract the 50 per cent. business relief if the value of the timber would have attracted business relief at the date of the death (assuming that the relevant provisions had then been in force).

Corporation Tax

Apportionment (Close companies)

FA 1978, ss.35, 36, Sch.5

Legal restrictions. In trying to prevent undistributed income from being apportioned, it cannot be argued that rules, governing the payment of dividends, which are contained in a company's articles of association, amount to restrictions imposed by law, Noble v. Laygate Investments Ltd, Ch.D. [1978] S.T.C. 430. The Statute is now in FA 1972, Sch.16, para.14.

Non-resident participators. By a Statement of Practice, the Board will accept exemption from UK tax on any apportioned income of a non-resident, whose dividend income is relieved from higher rates under a double taxation agreement (SP 1/78, see Simon's Tax Intelligence, 22 September 1978, p.456).

Requirements, acquisition of businesses—from 10 April 1978. For those trading companies or members of trading groups still left within the field of apportionment, further relief is given in that the cost of acquisition (including setting up) of the first business, or later acquiring an unconnected business, will rank as a requirement of the company's business and a reason for not distributing income.

The background to this is that the previous restriction was an anti-avoidance measure, but innocent acquisitions were penalised and the inability to include the need to repay a first business loan hit particularly hard.

The principal planning points are that: only trading companies or members of trading groups qualify, and costs of acquisition include costs of acquiring controlling shareholdings and repaying loan capital.

For anti-avoidance reasons, the relief will not usually apply to acquisitions from associated companies (current or at the end of the accounting period). (See FA 1978, Sch.5, para.2.)

It applies to liabilities existing after 10 April 1978, but which relate to earlier acquisitions. Thus old loans may now be repaid without fear of automatic apportionment.

Changes have been made for these purposes to what is meant by an associated company and an associate of a participator in control tests set out in FA 1978, Sch.5, para.2.

Thresholds raised—from 26 October 1977. For trading income of close trading companies only, abatement is on levels to £25,000 (fully abated) and to £75,000 (½ abatement of £75,000 *minus* the amount of estate or trading income).

This removes apportionment fears of most close trading companies, and those which have only trading income and no associates need be concerned about apportionment only if profits go above £45,402.

The associated companies restriction is now only in regard of trading associates which actually have traded at some time during the accounting period. This changed restriction does not apply to the associated companies provision for small companies rate.

The £500 limit for distributable investment income is raised to £1,000 in respect of accounting periods ending after 26 October 1977.

Community land transactions

FA 1978, s.34

From 6 April 1976, authorities, joint boards or body corporates, set up under the Community Land Act 1975, have now been granted corporation tax exemption on land transactions accounted for under that Act. Local authorities already had exemption.

Groups, replacement of business assets
TA 1970, s.276; FA 1965, s.33

> The Revenue take the view that to obtain the benefit of capital gains roll-over relief for companies within a group, the company making the gain or the qualifying replacement must be a member of a group and the company carrying out the complementary transaction must be a member of the same group *when that transaction is carried out*. The concept of "same group" is as defined in TA 1970, s.272(3). See also CCAB Press Release 10 January 1978, Simon's Tax Intelligence, 20 January 1978, p.25.

Small companies rate—from 26 October 1977
FA 1978, s.17

> The reduced rate of 42 per cent now applies to income where profits are below £50,000 (previously £40,000).
>
> There is marginal relief where profits are between £50,000 and £85,000 (previously £40,000 and £65,000) and the fraction is 1/7th.
>
> Remember that the limits of £50,000 and £85,000 are reduced where there are associated companies, see FA 1972, s.95(3)(4)(5).

Double Tax Treaties

New treaties and amendments to existing treaties
Treaties or amendments relating to the sea-bed and sub-soil
Official discussions
Notice of termination of certain treaties
Special points
United States: Exchange of information

The treaties referred to below are generally in respect of taxes on income and capital gains, unless otherwise specified.

New treaties or amendments to existing treaties were agreed and/or published as follows—

Austria	—amending protocol published as draft S.I. Not yet ratified.
Botswana	—new treaty published as S.I.1978 No. 183.
Canada	—new treaty not yet published in UK.
Cyprus	—amending protocol not yet ratified.
Denmark	—new treaty not yet ratified.
Ethiopia	—new treaty (air transport profits), published as S.I. 1977 No. 1297.
Gambia	—new treaty not yet ratified.
Ghana	—new treaty published as S.I.1978 No. 785.
Hungary	—new treaty published as S.I.1978 No. 1056.
India	—new treaty not yet ratified.
Ireland	—new treaty (deceased estates, inheritances and gifts) published as S.I.1978 No. 1107.
Jordan	—new treaty (shipping and air transport) published as draft S.I. Not yet ratified.
Korea	—new treaty published as S.I.1978 No. 786.
Luxembourg	—amending protocol published as draft S.I. Not yet ratified.
Malawi	—amendment published as draft S.I., not yet ratified.

Netherlands —new treaty (deceased estates and gifts) published as draft S.I., not yet ratified.

New Zealand—amendment, not yet ratified.

Norway —two amending protocols published as draft S.I.s; third protocol not yet signed.

Philippines —new treaty published as S.I.1978 No. 184.

Poland —new treaty published as S.I.1978 No. 282.

Singapore —amending protocol published as S.I.1978 No. 787.

South Africa —new treaty (deceased estates and gifts) published as draft S.I. Not yet ratified.

Sweden —new treaty not yet ratified.

Switzerland —new treaty published as S.I.1978 No. 1408.

United States—new treaty not yet ratified; third protocol not yet ratified.

—new treaty (deceased estates and gifts) published as draft S.I. Not yet ratified.

Venezuela —new treaty (shipping and air transport) published as draft S.I. Not yet ratified.

Treaties or amendments to treaties, expressed to contain provisions relating to the exploration and exploitation of the sea-bed and sub-soil and their natural resources, were published or discussed as follows:

Denmark —discussions (April 1978).

France —third protocol agreed but not yet signed (July 1978).

Netherlands —discussions (July 1978).

Norway —second amending protocol published as draft S.I.; third protocol awaiting signature.

Sweden —discussions (June 1978).

Official discussions have been held as follows:

Belgium —about a new Convention (February 1978).

Denmark —about a new Convention for deceased estates, inheritances and gifts (October 1978).

France —about a new Convention for deceased estates, inheritances and gifts (July 1978).

Guernsey ⎫ representations were invited in May in preparation for exploratory talks on a new Arrangement.
Isle of Man ⎬
Jersey ⎭

Notice of termination was given in respect of treaties with:

Canada	—(deceased estates) termination by the UK with effect from 30 September 1978 (see Simon's Tax Intelligence, 11 August 1978, p.366).
Nigeria	—termination by Nigeria with effect from 6 April 1979 for UK income tax and 1 January 1979 for corporation tax.

Special Points

Generally, the new treaties and amendments to treaties relating to taxes on income and capital gains, provide that in respect of dividends paid by UK companies, overseas shareholders (except for companies owning more than 10 per cent. of the paying company's voting power) are entitled to the UK tax credit reduced by income tax at 15 per cent. Withholding taxes on dividends, interest and royalties paid to UK residents are generally not to exceed 15 per cent. However, in the following circumstances, the rules vary.

Austria. Withholding tax on dividends from Austria to the UK only is restricted to 5 per cent. where paid to a 25 per cent. or more controlling company; however, in the case of Austrian withholding tax in this situation, whilst the highest Austrian corporation tax rate on distributed profits is more than 10 percentage points below the tax on undistributed profits, the rate is restricted to 10 per cent.

Botswana. Includes a tax-sparing clause.

Canada. Income tax text not yet published in UK. The Estate Duty treaty was terminated because it had no effect for the estates of persons dying after the end of 1971. The Inland Revenue has published a note explaining how Canadian income tax on capital gains deemed to arise on a person's death is dealt with for CTT purposes.

Ghana. In general, no withholding tax will be levied on dividends paid by Ghanaian companies to UK residents. The treaty includes a tax-sparing clause.

Hungary. Withholding tax on dividends is restricted to 5 per cent. where paid to a 25 per cent. or more controlling company. Interest and royalties are taxed in the recipient's country of residence unless he has a permanent establishment or fixed base in the other country. No ACT credit is given.

Ireland. (Deceased estates, inheritances and gifts). Each country is to give tax credit against its own tax if the "situs" of the property is in the other country. Where property is in a third country, the tax credit is given by the State having "subsidiary taxing rights"—i.e., where the deceased or the donor was domiciled (or deemed to be domiciled) in the other State. Special rules apply for settlements. Treaty covers CTT and Irish gift and inheritance taxes.

Korea. Withholding tax on dividends paid to a 10 per cent. or more controlling company is restricted to 10 per cent. which applies only for dividends from Korea to the UK, from the UK, 15 per cent.; on interest, it is restricted to 10 per cent. in the case of loans over two years; on industrial royalties, it is restricted to 10 per cent.

Luxembourg. Where dividends are paid to a Luxembourg 10 per cent. or more controlling company, that company will be entitled to one-half of the UK tax credit reduced by 5 per cent. of the aggregate of the dividend and the tax credit. Luxembourg withholding tax on dividends to a 25 per cent. or more controlling company is restricted to 5 per cent.

Malawi. Generally, there is no withholding tax on dividends paid by Malawi's companies to UK residents.

Philippines. The UK tax credit is restricted by income tax at 25 per cent. Philippines withholding tax on dividends to UK 10 per cent. or more controlling companies is restricted to 15 per cent., and to 25 per cent. in other cases. Withholding tax on interest paid by a company in respect of the public issue of bonds, etc., is restricted to 10 per cent. Withholding tax on certain film, etc., royalties, is restricted to 15 per cent., and to 25 per cent. in other cases.

Poland. Withholding tax on dividends to 10 per cent. or more controlling companies is restricted to 5 per cent. from Poland to the UK (from the UK it is 15 per cent.). Interest is taxed only in the recipient's country of residence unless he has a permanent establishment or fixed base in the other country. Withholding tax on royalties is restricted to 10 per cent.

Singapore. Dividends will be exempt from withholding tax. "Approved" interest and royalties are exempt from Singapore tax. There is a tax-sparing clause.

South Africa. (Deceased estates and gifts). The country in which the transferor was domiciled (or was domiciled within 10 years preceding the transfer) can tax property wherever it is situated. The other country may tax specified categories of property: immovable property, business property of a permanent establishment, etc.; both countries may tax property if the transferor was domiciled in neither country. The country in which the tranferor was not domiciled must, generally, give the tax credit; and the country of domicile must give tax credit for other country's tax on the specified categories of property.

Switzerland. Where dividends are paid to a Swiss 10 per cent. or more controlling company, that company will be entitled to one-half of the UK tax credit less 5 per cent. of the aggregate of the dividend and tax credit. Swiss withholding tax on dividends to a UK 25 per cent. or more controlling company is restricted to per cent.

United States. At time of going to press, a third amending protocol to the proposed 1975 treaty was awaiting signature and consideration by the US Senate which had declined to ratify the proposed new treaty (as amended by the 1976 and 1977 protocols) on the ground that it refused to compromise the rights of the individual states to tax multinational companies on a "unitary tax" basis—a basis which article 9(4) of the proposed treaty sought to prohibit.

At the time of going to press the text of the new treaty with Canada had not been published by HMSO and the texts were not available in respect of Denmark, Gambia, India, Netherlands and Sweden.

United States: Exchange of Information

A working arrangement was announced in March between the UK Inland Revenue and the US Internal Revenue Service in respect of the exchange of information relating to: multinational's intra-group transactions which *may* involve tax havens; new or apparent patterns or techniques of tax avoidance; and *the study of* transfer pricing practices.

Simultaneous examination (audit) procedures are laid down.

The working arrangement is made under the terms of the exchange of information provisions of the current (1945) double tax treaty. See 1977 Simon's Tax Intelligence, p.104.

The United States already has a simultaneous audit arrangement in operation with Canada.

Development Land Tax

Buildings used for industrial purposes—deferral of liability
DLTA 1976, s.19

Deferred liability does not crystallise if the relevant buildings are destroyed (say by fire) and are rebuilt, provided the trader does not go out of business and provided that a non-qualifying use is not positively established. Mere disuse pending rebuilding does not crystallise the DLT liability. Even if there is some temporary non-qualifying use of part of the site (and it would need to be for at least half of a two-year period to count) there is a "just and reasonable" limit to any liability, see DLT 1976, s.27(4). (CCAB clarification from the Inland Revenue, see Simon's Tax Intelligence, 14 July 1978, p.323.)

"In-house" costs
DLTA 1976, Sch.2, para.32

The "wholly and exclusively" rule is not interpreted by the Inland Revenue as excluding a reasonable proportion of "in-house" costs such as architects' departments.

41

Interest on unpaid tax and payments in advance
DLTA 1976, s.47(1)

The Income Tax (Interest on Unpaid Tax) Order 1974, S.I. 1974 No. 966 which increased the prescribed rate of interest on overdue tax from 6 per cent. to 9 per cent. as from 1 July 1976 does not apply to unpaid or overpaid DLT.

For DLT the rate is 6 per cent. Where interest has already been paid at the higher rate, the excess will be refunded, together with interest at 6 per cent. on that excess. No steps will be taken to recover any excess amount of interest paid by the Inland Revenue to taxpayers. (See Inland Revenue Press release, Simon's Tax Intelligence, 15 September 1978, p.452.)

Options granted before 13 September 1974
DLTA 1976, s.45(6)

The Inland Revenue in practice treat as not liable to DLT, a disposal in accordance with an option granted before 13 September 1974 to acquire at a fixed price. (CAAB clarification obtained from the Inland Revenue, see Simon's Tax Intelligence, 14 July 1978, p.323.)

"Pre-sale" arrangements
DLTA 1976, Sch.2 amended by FA 1977, s.55

Where there is an outright sale of land on the basis that the vendor is required to carry out work at a future date the sale price can be apportioned accordingly even if the cost of the future work cannot be exactly quantified at the time of the sale. (CCAB clarification from the Inland Revenue, see Simon's Tax Intelligence, 14 July 1978, pp.321 and 322.)

Reduced rate
DLTA 1976, s.13 amended by FA 1978, s.76

The interim period, during which DLT on realised development value up to a figure of £150,000 in any one year is to be charged at the lower rate of 66⅔ per cent. rather than 80 per cent., is to continue until 31 March 1980 instead of 31 March 1979.

"Six-year" rule
DLTA 1976, ss.5(6), 12(4), 12(5)(*b*), 13(4) and 20(1)

The £10,000 exemption and the £150,000 reduced rate band are available on a disposal outside the group by a group company of land which it acquired from another group company after 12 September 1974 and within six years of the date of disposal. However, these reliefs are not available where a company acquires land from another group company and disposes of it externally within twelve months of the original acquisition by the group. (CCAB clarification from the Inland Revenue, see Simon's Tax Intelligence, 14 July 1978, pp.321 and 322.)

Schedule D, Cases I and II

Assessment of profits

Willingale v. Int. Comm. Bank Ltd. H.L. [1978] S.T.C. 75

> In this case, it was reaffirmed that accountancy principles cannot override established tax principles. More importantly, the decision affects the timing of when tax is payable, in that whilst profits are accruing but cannot be realised, such anticipated profits are not assessable.

Car leasing

Simon's Tax Intelligence, 4 August 1978, p.361

> *Background.* Traditional car leasing contracts running for two or three years, used an estimate of the open market value of the car at the end of the lease in calculating the rent payable. When the car was sold, there would be a final adjustment if the car realised more or less than the estimated market value. The lessor was given tax relief for the depreciation borne and the lessee had tax relief on the net rentals paid.
>
> However, the Inland Revenue are taking a different view of non-traditional leasing arrangements whereby rentals are calculated using a residual value (sometimes a purely nominal value is used) of less than the expected open market value of

the car at the end of the lease, and the car is eventually sold to a person connected with the lessee for that figure who thus acquires the car for less than its market value.

The Inland Revenue are considering applying, to leases of this kind, certain taxation provisions which are not normally relevant to traditional leases. As far as the lessor is concerned, the car may be considered to be stock-in-trade rather than an asset qualifying for capital allowances. If capital allowances are given, the provisions of FA 1971, s.44(6)(*b*) may be applied so that the open market value, rather than the sale proceeds, of the car, is brought into the tax computation at the end of the lease.

Also, the lessee's rental payments may be disallowed, in whole or in part, under TA 1970, ss.130(*a*) and 130(*f*), as not being made "wholly and exclusively" for the purposes of the business or as being, in part, capital expenditure.

The person connected with the lessee who acquires the car, may be liable under the provisions of Schedule E on any benefit he obtains, or under TA 1970, s.492 *et seq.*, if the car is sold.

The open market value should be taken to be the trade price rather than showroom price.

Contingencies
I.R. Comrs. v. Titaghur Jute Factory Ltd. C.S. [1978] S.T.C. 166

It is important to ensure the *accurate* measurement of future liabilities in order to secure a tax deduction for annual provisions made to meet such obligations. In the case, a deduction of a measured sum was allowed in the year in which statute imposed the liability for the future payments on the firm even though earlier years were taken into account in making the provision.

Divers and diving supervisors
FA 1978, s.29

Because of the large numbers of divers working full time for single employers in the North Sea oil and gas extraction industry, but retaining their self-employed status and taking large sums of money in fees, they were brought within the PAYE net by FA 1976. This was principally an anti-avoidance measure. However, the tax consequences were threatening to send divers and diving supervisors abroad to other operational areas and the Schedule D basis was therefore imposed for 1978-79 onwards, on all divers working in the North Sea, subject to safeguards.

Planning points.   Although in employment, the performance of the duties is treated as the carrying on of a trade, deemed to have commenced on the 6 April 1978.

Diving operations in the UK or areas designated under the Continental Shelf Act 1964, s.1(7), mainly the UK area of the North Sea, are covered by this measure.

The Revenue must be informed of payments made to those concerned.

Non-domiciled divers who qualified for the 50 per cent. Schedule E deduction will be worse off under Schedule D but there is no option between the two Schedules.

Administrative arrangements are being made to cover divers working in both designated and non-designated areas where there would be Schedule D and Schedule E liability, subject to double taxation treaties.

Farming and market gardening
FA 1978, s.28

Outline.   From 1977-78 or later years of assessment, where the difference between the profits for two consecutive years is 30 per cent. or more, the farmer can claim for those two years' profits to be averaged between each of the years of assessment. Marginal relief operates for differences amounting to between 25 per cent. and 30 per cent.

Planning points.   The relief is only applicable to sole traders and partnerships, not companies.

The measure of profits to be averaged is for each year of assessment (and not for the basis period). Profits are those before capital allowances, stock relief and losses.

Losses are treated as nil profits and will remain available for relief under the appropriate provisions of the Taxes Act.

For partnerships, claims must be made by all partners who are individuals, jointly (but not company partners).

In commencement or cessation, averaging is not available for profits of the first year or the last year of trade or where partnership changes are treated as cessations. Elections for continuation would enable relief to be obtained during partnership changes.

Claims must be made within two years of the end of the second year of assessment, but can be revoked if the assessment is not final and conclusive.

The adjustments are ignored for TA 1970, s.118(1)(b) (discontinuance) and for computing relevant income for stock relief purposes.

Earlier claims for stock relief and capital allowances need to be taken into account when contemplating a claim for averaging, but they may not be withdrawn if assessments are final and conclusive. The Revenue is to consider the difficulties arising on this.

Where a decision to make or revoke a wife's earnings election turns on later years' income, the Board already has discretion to extend the time limit.

Losses in early years of trade
FA 1978, s.30

Background. It is common for losses to be made in the first years of a trade, whether because of capital allowances or other commercial causes. New carry-back provisions enable a trader to have tax relief early, by repayment of tax, by allowing losses to be set against *other* income of *earlier* years.

Outline. An individual who is in business, either on his own or in partnership, can claim to have his losses for his first year or subsequent three years set against his other income of the preceding three years.

Planning points. Only initial trading losses of unincorporated businesses qualify.

The relief covers trades, professions and vocations but not woodlands.

It is an alternative to other reliefs and there can be no double allowance.

The first year of loss to which the relief can apply is 1978-79.

Claims are to be made within two years of the year of assessment in which the loss was sustained.

The trade, etc., must be carried on on a commercial basis with a reasonable expectation of profits.

The calculation of the loss is as for TA 1970, s.168, to include capital allowances and stock relief.

A re-commencement (except partnership changes) does not qualify for relief.

The anti-avoidance exclusions of TA 1970, s.168 relief apply to this relief in respect of schemes of leasing, commodity futures, and transfers to connected persons.

Partnership losses are apportioned between partners in the usual way.

A husband or wife joining each other's business would not constitute a trade being newly carried on, unless the business has been going no longer than the period to which the relief applies.

Taking over a business from an unconnected person would be a trade, etc., newly carried on. Similarly a partner who has a loss in his first year as a partner can claim the new relief.

Relief is not given against income from oil extraction activities nor from purchase and sale of securities by persons other than dealers.

A Case V trade loss is to be relieved but only against other Case V income and after a 25 per cent. deduction from the loss.

Stock and work-in-progress

Long-term contracts. By concession, any uplift, resulting from revised valuations under SSAP 9 of long-term contracts, is to be excluded from tax computations. Stock relief will not be restricted (The CCAB Press Release, 26 April 1978 and the full text of SSAP 9 are reproduced in Simon's Tax Intelligence, 12 May 1978, p.216).

Stock relief. This is to continue indefinitely, but with legislation to come in 1979 to limit the build-up of deferred tax liabilities. The government intends "to build into the present stock relief scheme provisions to write off so much of the relief as remains after a six-year period" (extract from a speech by Rt. Hon. Joel Barnett, M.P., on 4 December 1978 to the Institute of Chartered Accountants' Conference on Deferred Taxation). See also in Forward Notes under *Stock relief.*

In respect of building licences, granted under the Community Land Act 1975, for stock relief purposes, the cost of the licence will qualify for stock relief as work in progress provided that substantial development on the underlying land has begun. (See SP 8/78 reproduced in Simon's Tax Intelligence, 24 November 1978, p.542.)

Valuation changes. Notwithstanding the Willingale case (see above), a trader can attribute a fair share of accrued profits on long-term contracts, to work-in-progress, but on a change of basis any difference is not spread but assessable in the year after the change (Pearce v. Woodhall Duckham Ltd. C.A. [1978] S.T.C. 372).

Trade carried on abroad
Newstead v. Frost Ch.D. [1978] S.T.C. 239

In the Newstead v. Frost case, which dealt with the commercial nature of a tax avoidance partnership, it is interesting to note that once it is established that income comes from a valid foreign partnership the decision (H. L.) in Colquhoun v. Brooks (2 T.C. 490) applies, and the income is assessable under Case V, as income from foreign possessions, and not Case I, even where carried on by a UK resident. The Inland Revenue are seeking to challenge that decision and Newstead v. Frost will thus go to the Lords. (For C.A. decision see Simon's Tax Intelligence, 21 July 1978, p.335.)

Trade, etc., carried on partly abroad
FA 1978, s.27 and Sch.4

Background. The government had been under pressure to introduce reliefs for the self-employed to correspond with the measures already in force in respect of employees who work partly abroad. The Inland Revenue is not sympathetic to the concept of this relief either in respect to employers or the self-employed, and the rules are very strictly adhered to.

Outline.   From 1978-79, individuals who are resident in the UK and who, either singly or in partnership, carry on a trade, profession or vocation can claim relief in respect of business absences from the UK on at least 30 qualifying days in the year of assessment.

Planning points.   The relief is 25 per cent. of the individual's relevant income from the trade, etc., which is chargeable for the year of assessment to which the qualifying days of absence relate.

Therefore it is

$$25\% \times \frac{\text{days'absence}}{\text{days of trading}} \times \text{relevant income}$$

Relevant income is profit assessed for the year after capital allowances and stock relief but before loss relief.

Absences in basis period. This concept does not present problems for commencement and cessation periods, particularly in the assessment of partnerships, see below, as it is absences in the year of assessment that give the relief and which are used in its computation.

No 100 per cent. relief is available for 365 days' absence as is available for Schedule E.

Qualifying days.   For the 30-day limit, all qualifying days of all trades, etc., carried on are to be totalled. It does not matter whether the days' absences run on or are on separate occasions. A qualifying day is defined as a day absent from the UK when time is substantially devoted to the activities of the trade, etc., or one of at least seven days' consecutive absence substantially for the trade activities, or one spent travelling wholly and exclusively for the purposes of the trade.

The dual purpose rule would apply to travel which is partly for trade, etc., and partly, say, for a holiday. Absent from the UK means absent at the end of the day. For example, self-employed fishermen who make no calls at foreign ports would not qualify.

The day of departure but not the day of return counts as a day absent.

An oil rig in the North Sea is not a place abroad.

Partnerships.   An individual partner's relief is calculated on his absences and on his income from the partnership, calculated as above. This is so even if the partnership is treated as ceasing and recommencing, or where he ceases to belong to the partnership. Partners can make adjustments so that the tax savings are shared.

The resident partner of a partnership controlled abroad will be eligible for relief only on absences in respect of the UK end of the trade, etc.

Class IV NIC. No deduction is made for this relief in computing Class IV NIC profits.

Retirement annuities. No deduction is made for this relief in computing net relevant earnings for retirement annuity relief.

Trading receipts

Two cases shed further light on whether profits from land sales are trading income.

Where there is a definite intention, going beyond a mere contingent hope, of building up a permanent investment suitable, say, for a property investment company, but *bona fide* changed circumstances necessitate subsequent sale, the surplus on disposal of the property concerned would not be a trading receipt (Simons v. I.R. Comrs. and others Ch.D. [1978] S.T.C. 344).

However, where a builder, aware of the development potential of certain land, attempted to transfer the beneficial interest to his wife and a nominee, the eventual large sale proceeds were nonetheless ruled as trading receipts (Smart v. Lowndes Ch.D., Simon's Tax Intelligence, 14 July 1978, p.324).

Schedule E

Benefits: cars
         loans
         scholarships
         season tickets
         thresholds raised
Directors' loan accounts
Divers and diving supervisors
Foreign agencies
Profit-sharing schemes
Redundancy

Benefits

Cars.   From 6 April 1978 a new table of cash equivalents of car benefits came into force under S.I. 1978 No. 434.

CAR BENEFITS ASSESSABLE 1978–79

CARS UP TO £8,000†

	Business use over 25,000 miles a year (Other cases—shown in brackets)	
	Under 4 yrs. old*	*4 or more yrs. old**
A. 1,300 c.c. or less	£95 (£190)	£65 (£130)
B. 1,301 c.c.–1,800 c.c.	£125 (£250)	£85 (£165)
C. More than 1,800 c.c.	£190 (£380)	£130 (£255)
CARS ABOVE £8,000†		
£8,001–£12,000	£275 (£550)	£185 (£365)
£12,000 upwards	£440 (£880)	£295 (£585)

CARS WITHOUT A CYLINDER CAPACITY—in A. B. and C. delete the c.c. references and substitute:

    A.   up to £2,500†
    B.   £2,500–£3,499†
    C.   £3,500–£8,000†

*At the relevant year of assessment
†That is the original market value

Loans. For beneficial loan arrangements, the prescribed rate was fixed by S.I. 1978, No. 28 at 9 per cent. in respect of the rules in FA 1976, s.66 and Sch.8, as from 6 April 1978 (Simon's Tax Intelligence, 3 February 1978, p.36).

The Inland Revenue propose to extend extra-statutory concession A6 (removal expenses) so as not to charge to tax under FA 1976, s.66 (cheap loans), the benefit on a "cheap" bridging loan from an employer which is in excess of £25,000 (the level at which such interest is not eligible for relief) provided–
(a) the loan is made where the employee has had to change his residence as the result of a transfer within his employer's organisation, or in order to take up a new employment; and
(b) the loan is outstanding for no more than 12 months (or such longer period as the Board may allow).
See Simon's Tax Intelligence, 15 December 1978, p.564.

Scholarships. Where an employer sets up and finances an arrangement under which scholarships are awarded to the children of directors or higher paid employees, the Revenue have contended that those awards give rise to assessable benefits.

However, where the scheme is open to all (i.e. the public at large) and an award *happens* to go to the child of a higher paid employee, the Revenue will not contend that an assessable benefit arises.

The scholarships concerned are for all types of education; school, university or other. (Press Releases at Simon's Tax Intelligence, 23 June 1978, p.276 and 30 June 1978, p.303.)

Season tickets. If an employer reimburses or otherwise meets the cost of travelling to work, there is liability under general Schedule E rules. However, if an employer contracts with British Rail to provide his employee with a season ticket which cannot be converted into cash in the employee's hands and the employee *is not a director or higher paid employee,* there is no liability on the value of the season ticket since it does not represent the meeting of pecuniary liability, nor is it convertible into cash (House of Commons Written Answers, reproduced in Simon's Tax Intelligence, 16 June 1978, p.255 and 8 December 1978, p.556).

Thresholds raised. The earnings threshold above which the special rules for taxing benefits in kind contained in FA 1976, ss.60–72 apply, is increased from £7,500 to £8,500 with effect from 1979–80 (FA 1978, s.23).

Directors' loan accounts

Gorforth v. Newsmith Stainless Ltd, Ch.D., see Simon's Tax Intelligence, 1 December 1978, p.551.

> An amount credited to a director's account in the books of a company constitutes 'payment' of that sum and tax is deductible under PAYE.

Divers and diving supervisors

FA 1978, s.29

> From 1978–79 onwards, divers and diving supervisors are taxed under Schedule D, Case I, and not Schedule E. This covers operations in the UK or in a designated area of the continental shelf, and is of main application to the UK North Sea area (see also p.45 for further details).

Foreign agencies: temporary workers

Simon's Tax Intelligence, 14 April 1978, p.153

> It was suggested that the rules of F(No. 2)A 1975, s.38 (PAYE on agency workers) would not apply where the agency was not resident in the UK. However, the Revenue have made it clear that it is the UK employer of such a worker who is responsible for PAYE tax and National Insurance Contributions.

Profit sharing schemes

FA 1978, ss.53–61

> *Outline.* With effect from 6 April 1979, employee participants of an approved scheme can be allocated shares in their company (up to £500 worth per annum per employee) with no Schedule E charge on the benefit obtained.

> The company will provide funds to the scheme trustees, and employee participants must undertake not to dispose of the shares for five years.

> After that, there will be some Schedule E liability on a sliding scale for years 5 to 10, but there will be no liability if the shares are held for ten years, or where shares are appropriated on the cessation of employment through injury, disability, redun-

dancy, death, or reaching pensionable age for social security purposes. On any increase in value of the shares over the market value at the time of appropriation, the participants will be liable for capital gains tax in the normal way.

Planning points. Each scheme will be administered entirely by a trust set up by the company, using funds from the company to buy shares in it or its parent.

Contributions by the company to the trustees will be allowable deductions for corporation tax purposes, as would further sums paid to the trustees to meet, for instance, a CGT liability. The trustees must use such sums within nine months of the end of the period of account in which the company charges them as an expense.

Money provided by a close company for the purchase of shares by trustees will not be treated as distributions.

Difficulties in respect of UK subsidiaries of foreign corporations are surmountable by using the parent's shares.

Eligible employees are defined at FA 1978, Sch.9, paras. 2, 9–11.

The relevant shares are as defined at FA 1978, Sch.9, paras. 5–8, 16, 17.

The trustees are not liable to additional rate tax on dividends received on shares as under FA 1973, s.16.

Charge to tax will be in the following circumstances:—
1. Shares appropriated to employee — no charge.
2. Disposal will give a Schedule E charge on the employee a percentage of the locked in value (defined FA 1978, s.53(4) and s.55(2)) dependent on the period held (see FA 1978, ss.54(7) and 55(1)).
3. Any excess (above £500 p.a.) or unauthorised (to ineligible persons) shares are chargeable to Schedule E on market value at the earliest of: 10th anniversary of appropriation date or disposal or death.
4. Capital receipts may be chargeable on the employee for the year in which the trustees become entitled: certain items are excluded (FA 1978, ss.56, 57).
5. Rights issues. Where the disposal includes shares acquired, by payment by the participator, from a rights issue, the disposal proceeds are reduced by the proportion of any consideration paid for the rights issues which, immediately

before the disposal, the market value of the shares disposed of bears to the market value of all the shares held by the trustees at that time. No account is taken of consideration paid out of the proceeds from a disposal of rights; this provides a form of roll-over. (See rules at FA 1978, ss.55(4), (5) and 56(3).)

6. In general, there is no liability on company reconstructions, amalgamations and takeovers, which the legislation leap-frogs.
7. Capital gains tax will be payable on the value of disposals in excess of the capital gains market value at the appropriation date.
8. All Schedule E liability will be collected through an imposed PAYE regime.

Redundancy and other payments for loss of employment
FA 1978, s.24

The exemption is raised from £5,000 to £10,000 from 6 April 1978 and is designed to encourage workers receiving redundancy or severance payments, to accept other jobs by removing the prospect of large tax liabilities on the lump sums received.

An anti-avoidance measure plugs the loophole whereby employees could waive rights to commute their pensions into a tax-free lump-sum and in return receive a larger lump-sum, tax free. This applies from 17 May 1978.

Tax avoidance

[Note: for CTT avoidance, see pp.26 *et seq.*]

Annuity sold for lump sum

> FA 1977, s.48 put an end to the kind of avoidance scheme used in the case of I.R. Comrs. v. Plummer C.A. [1978] S.T.C. 517 (and see Parliamentary Answer reported in Simon's Tax Intelligence, 9 June 1978, p.252).

Beneficial ownership

Burman v. Hedges & Butler Ch.D., Simon's Tax Intelligence, 1 December 1978, p.550

> In a scheme involving the formation of companies, transfer of shares and a voluntary liquidation, it was held that it cannot be said that the taxpayer company did not have the beneficial ownership of those shares because there was nothing to prevent it parting with the shares. In addition, the contention that one of the companies involved was acting as agent or nominee for another company involved in the scheme was rejected as being wholly without foundation in fact.

Commercial transactions

Certain tax cases revolving around the *bona fide* commerciality of transactions have been decided in favour of the taxpayer and illustrate criteria that are applied in testing whether the commercial or the avoidance inspiration is the greater.

A transaction carried out to improve a livelihood is carried out for *bona fide* commercial reasons. There is no requirement for the commercial reasons to be directly connected with the taxpayer's interest in the companies concerned, but can be in something separate to which the transaction advantageously contributes, Clark v. I.R. Comrs. Ch.D. [1978] S.T.C. 614 (see also under Transactions in securities).

A genuine commercial objective cannot be ignored "simply because the machinery used to achieve it was adopted solely for fiscal purposes". A taxpayer has a right to organise his business affairs to minimise tax liability. Newstead v. Frost Ch.D. [1978] S.T.C. 239 at 251.

A suspicion that a transaction is a paper sham damages a taxpayer's position in seeking to establish commerciality, Williams v. I.R. Comrs. Ch.D. [1978] S.T.C. 379.

Commodity futures
FA 1978, s.31

Relief is not given under TA 1970, s.168 or 177(2) or FA 1978, s.30 in respect of a loss sustained in a trade, carried on by a partnership including a company, of dealing in commodity futures, if the arrangements are such that the sole or main benefit accruing would be a reduction in tax liability. Schemes effected or arrangements made after 5 April 1976 are caught.

Debt on a security
W. T. Ramsay Ltd. v. I.R. Comrs. Ch.D. [1978] S.T.C. 253

For there to be a debt on security, there must be a "security", an essential feature of which is a marketable security in the form of a document issued by the debtor. The losses created by the use of loans were not allowable.

Disposal of assets
Floor v. Davis C. A. [1978] S.T.C. 436

In an arranged scheme, whereby value passed out of shares in a company owned by the vendors of those shares, but where there had been a series of steps and acquisition of control, the final winding-up was nevertheless a disposal under FA 1965, Sch.7, para.15(2). For that statute, persons can exercise control.

For the case of Aberdeen Construction Group Ltd. v. I.R. Comrs. H.L. [1978] S.T.C. 127, see pp.16 and 17.

Double taxation and avoidance

There is now a UK/US working arrangement for the exchange of information to prevent fiscal evasion and to administer statutory provisions against legal avoidance (see Simon's Tax Intelligence, 10 March 1978, p.104), and p.40.

Extra statutory concessions
Vestey v. I.R. Comrs. (No. 2) Ch.D. [1978] S.T.C. 567

A powerful indictment of the system of extra-statutory concessions was made in the Vestey No. 2 case, with a pointer as to their application: "I, in company with many judges before me, am totally unable to understand on what basis the Inland Revenue Commissioners are entitled to make extra-statutory concessions . . . But even if . . . extra-statutory concessions are permissible and do form part of our tax code, nevertheless they do represent a published code, which applies indifferently to all those who fall, or who can bring themselves within, its scope", Walton J. at p.575.

Industrial buildings
FA 1978, s.37(6)

For anti-avoidance measures connected with the application of industrial buildings allowances to long leases, see p.12.

Land sales with rights to repurchase
FA 1978, s.32

Relief for premiums under TA 1970, s.83 (deductions from rents) or s.134 (deductions to traders for 'notional' rents) is denied, where a charge arises under TA 1970, s.82, where land is sold with right to repurchase. The section applies from 2 December 1976.

Legislation

Retrospective legislation. The Chancellor in his Budget Statement 1978 had this to say on the subject of tax avoidance:

> "This has emerged recently in a new form which involves marketing a succession of highly artificial schemes—when one is detected, the next is immediately sold—and is accompanied by a level of secrecy which amounts almost to conspiracy to mislead. The time has come not only to stop the particular schemes we know about but to ensure that no schemes of a similar nature can be marketed in future."

The attack on the tax system by avoidance scheme devisers has made use of the custom of Parliament legislating only from the date on which a warning to legislate was given and by cloaking the highly artificial transactions in great secrecy. Retrospective legislation counters this.

It seems like that retrospective legislation will be the 'thing of the future'. Rather than blanket anti-avoidance provisions under which innocent tax planning devices could be caught, as soon as the Revenue learns of artificial schemes, they will be specifically legislated against with retroactive force.

Persons who seek to maximise tax efficiency are not intended to be affected, but those who participate in specially devised schemes which make no commercial sense, in which the only cost is the fee to the scheme seller, will be hit.

Interpretation. It is only where the words are absolutely incapable of a construction which will accord with the apparent intention of the provision and will avoid a wholly unreasonable result, that the words of the enactment must prevail, (from Luke v. I.R. Comrs. 40 T.C. 630 at 646 quoted in Berry v. Warnett Ch.D. [1978] S.T.C. 504 at 516).

Penal legislation is to be construed extremely strictly, (Vestey v. I.R. Comrs. (No. 2) Ch.D. [1978] S.T.C. 567 at p.576).

Loss of employment payments
FA 1978, s.24(2), (4)

This section counters a device whereby an employee waives his rights to commute part of his pension for a tax-free lump sum, draws his pension in full and is awarded an *ex gratia* payment equal to, or larger than, the sum he would otherwise have received.

Previously such a payment would not have affected the amount of standard capital superannuation benefit; now it must be deducted from the amount of that benefit in the same way as lump sums awarded under superannuation schemes. The effect of this amendment is to bring such payments into charge to tax. It affects any payment which is treated as income received after 16 May 1978.

Losses allowable for capital gains tax
Eilbeck v. Rawling Ch.D., Simon's Tax Intelligence, 20 October 1978, p.481

Under FA 1965, Sch.6, para.4(1)(*a*), for expenditure to be allowable, it must be given "wholly and exclusively" for the asset. Where a payment was for the acquisition of an entire tax avoidance scheme (using reversionary interests in settlements), it is not wholly and exclusively for the asset in question and cannot be deducted.

Partnerships
Newstead v. Frost Ch.D. [1978] S.T.C. 239

Partnerships can be entered into by a company to exploit an individual's talent and to secure fiscal advantage and such aims do not necessarily invalidate the partnership (for C.A. Simon's Tax Intelligence, 21 July 1978, p.335).

Professional etiquette in tax avoidance schemes

The Bar Council has approved the following ruling: "Where counsel has advised a particular lay client on a tax avoidance scheme, he cannot subsequently appear against that client in proceedings relating to the same matter, whether such client be a finance house operating the scheme or an individual customer.

Where counsel has advised a finance house on such a scheme and the finance house has subsequently "sold" the scheme to its customers, or where counsel has advised a customer on the scheme, there is no objection in principle to counsel appearing against one or more of those customers (other, of course, than a customer whom counsel advised), in proceedings relating to the same scheme. There may, however, be particular circumstances in which it would be improper for counsel to act, or where counsel would be entitled to refuse to act on the ground of possible embarrassment. For example, in advising on a scheme for a finance house or for a customer, counsel may have acquired information which would lead him to suggest to the Revenue lines of inquiry that otherwise might not have occurred to them, in particular his knowledge of the background of the scheme might lead him to advise the Revenue in proceedings before the Special Commissioners to apply for an order for discovery.

Subject to the above, counsel should always bear in mind the importance of upholding the principle that, save in special circumstances, a barrister is bound to accept any brief in the Courts in which he professes to practise at a proper professional fee dependent on the length and difficulty of the case". (Taxation, July 15, 1978.)

Transactions in securities

Schemes which failed.   Share exchanges, to enable asset-stripping by payment of a dividend, where those shares could have been received in a taxable way, are within TA 1970, s.461 D and s.460 applies to the tax advantage, Anysz v. I.R. Comrs. Ch.D. [1978] S.T.C. 296. Those sections apply where schemes involve the use of interest-free loans made to the taxpayers, in addition to the share exchanges, Williams & Others v. I.R. Comrs. Ch.D. [1978] S.T.C. 379. A scheme is to be looked at as a whole in determining whether or not a tax advantage has been obtained and if there is another way in which profits could have reached the taxpayers, say by distribution of the profits by dividends, a tax advantage has arisen, I.R. Comrs. v. Wiggins Ch.D., Simon's Tax Intelligence, 8 December 1978, p.556.

Schemes which succeeded.   The crucial date for TA 1970, s.461 D, is the date of distribution of profits and not the date the taxpayer receives the proceeds of sale of shares. It was at the former date that the control test was applied and the transaction was deemed to be outside s.461 D. The transaction cannot be caught by s.461 C if the word "whereby" is taken to mean "by which" and not "by means of which" and on the facts the sale of shares was not the transaction directly giving an abnormal receipt by way of dividend, I.R. Comrs. v. Garvin, Ch.D, Simon's Tax Intelligence, 29 September 1978, p.461.

Where there are good commercial reasons and the main object is not the obtaining of a tax advantage, the transaction falls within the escape clause of TA 1970, s.460(1), Clark v. I.R. Comrs, Ch.D, Simon's Tax Intelligence, 3 November 1978, p.514.

Evidence.   To satisfy TA 1970, s.460(1)(*a*), the Revenue must adduce all evidence which is required to satisfy the Special Commissioners that the specified event has happened, I.R. Comrs. v. Garvin (see above).

Under s.460(6) the Commissioners do not have to disclose to the taxpayer why they believe the section applies to him, nor is there any requirement of natural justice that the taxpayer should have the right to reply to the Commissioners' counter statement under s.460(7), Balen v. I.R. Comrs. C.A. [1978] S.T.C. 420.

New clearance procedure.   The Revenue has undertaken for a trial period of 12 months to give reasons for refusing clearance but only where the applicants give a full account of each major part of the proposed transactions. (CCAB TR 290, 8 June 1978.)

Transfer of assets abroad
Vestey v. I.R. Comrs. (No. 2) Ch.D. [1978] S.T.C. 567 and Vestey v. I.R. Comrs. Ch.D. [1977] S.T.C. 415 (Vestey No. 1)

The Vestey No. 2 case (which is going to the House of Lords) has shown that beneficiaries of a discretionary trust are not (to date) to be taxed on income to which they are mere potential beneficiaries but have no right for it to be paid to them. In such circumstances there is no right under which there is power to enjoy the income of the trust fund within what is now TA 1970, s.478(1). Furthermore, income, under what is now TA 1970, s.478(5)(*d*), does not for the purposes of s.478(1) include accumulations of income which had been capitalised. Money paid to the taxpayer was therefore capital in the hands of the trustees and accordingly, the question of the taxpayer having any power to enjoy income, within s.478(1) did not arise.

Transfer of property, retention of life interest
Berry v. Warnett, Ch.D. [1978] S.T.C. 504

Market value cannot be substituted where the parties to an arrangement are at arm's length, and a settlor and trustee of a settlement are not connected persons, unless there is an element of bounty in the settlement.

Value Added Tax

Bad debt relief

FA 1978, s.12 and S.I. 1978 No. 1129

A limited relief is available in respect of accounting for input tax on supplies to customers who, before paying, become insolvent after 1 October 1978.

Planning points.   The claimant must have proved the insolvency to the extent only of the debt *excluding* the value added tax. The following evidence must be obtained: a certificate showing the amount proved in the insolvency; a copy of the tax invoice(s) or specified evidence; and records showing that tax was accounted for to the Commissioners.

There are detailed rules concerning preservation of records, offsets between debtors and creditors, determining the tax element of partly paid debts and repayment of relief.

The Tribunal case of Peter Cripwell & Associates CAR/78/131 held that credit notes cancelling bills to insolvent customers are invalid.

Business—definition

C. E. Comrs. v. Morrison's Academy Boarding Home Association [1978] S.T.C. 1

A "business" consists of making taxable supplies to con-

64

sumers in a continuous and business-like way, and profit-motive is irrelevant, thus, the VAT will encompass activities which otherwise might be considered non-commercial.

Penalties and nil returns

Keogh v. Gordon Q.B.D. [1978] S.T.C. 340

> Failure to submit a tax return is an offence FA 1972, s.38(7), even if the return due would be a "nil return".

Pension funds

Linotype and Machinery Ltd. v. C. & E. Comrs., MAN/78/4

> **Where a company and its pension fund trustees are different persons, the company cannot obtain input tax credit for administration expenses, even where it has a contractual liability to pay them, although it may obtain relief for tax incurred in setting up the pension fund.**

Registration and de-registration thresholds

FA 1978, s.11(1),(2)

> From 12 April 1978 the registration thresholds are increased to: *(a)* future limit—£10,000; *(b)* historical limit—£3,500 (1 quarter), £6,000 (2 quarters), £8,500 (3 quarters) and £10,000 (4 quarters).

> From 1 July 1978 the de-registration reference limits are increased thus: *(a)* future limit is £8,500 for the ensuing year; *(b)* historical limits for the past two-year period are £8,500 or less for each year or £2,500 or less for each quarter.

> *Planning points.* Before de-registering consider: will the inability to recover input tax make the business uncompetitive? Will claw-back of input tax on stock and assets held at de-registration create financial problems?

Written rulings

Hansard, 21 July 1978, col.426

> Where a customs officer in possession of the full facts gives an unequivocal written ruling or is proved to have misled a trader to that trader's detriment, the Commissioners will assess tax only from the date the trader is informed of the correct position.

> *Planning point*—obtain written rulings whenever possible.

Miscellaneous

Accounts examination
CCAB and Inland Revenue meeting June 1978

In respect of the procedures for examination of taxpayers' accounts introduced at the beginning of 1977, the Inland Revenue have reiterated that selection of accounts for in-depth examination by inspectors of taxes is not on a random basis, and that accountants should be given the opportunity to settle preliminary enquiries before an interview with the tax-payer is held; but local inspectors cannot be expected to provide an advance list of questions to be asked, and experience has shown that an early interview is usually the most economical way to achieve a speedy settlement.

Notes of interview should normally be made available to the accountant by inspectors if this is agreed in advance. It is not the Revenue's aim to seek an increase in taxable profits in all cases under enquiry, and in particular, they do not seek to apply notional gross profit rates; lists of such percentages are not circulated to inspectors.

For full notes of the matters discussed at the meeting, see Simon's Tax Intelligence, 10 November 1978, pp.516-524.

Back duty
Johnson v. Scott C.A. [1978] S.T.C. 476

For the purposes of TMA 1970, s.37 (Neglect: income tax and capital gains tax) the Crown does not have to establish the precise amounts of income which it is thought that the tax-payer has failed to declare. It merely has to establish neglect, i.e. that the figures put forward by the taxpayer are inadequate.

Interest on loans applied in acquiring an interest in a close company
FA 1974, Sch.1, para.10

Where a person has obtained relief from income tax in respect of interest on a loan applied in acquiring any part of the ordinary share capital of a close company or in lending on for use in the business of that or an associated company, the statutory provisions are to be interpreted as not requiring the company to remain close at the time of paying the interest. (See Statement of Practice SP 3/78 reproduced in Simon's Tax Intelligence, 27 October 1978, p.497.)

Personal reliefs
TA 1970, ss.12, 13, 17 and 18 amended by FA 1978, s.19

Apart from increases in reliefs, the following amendments were made by FA 1978, s.19—

(*a*) a housekeeper for TA 1970, s.12 may be a male but no housekeeper relief will be available if the male housekeeper has been allowed the married relief;

(*b*) the relief under TA 1970, s.13 can be claimed in respect of any relative, male or female, taking charge of an unmarried person's young brother or sister;

(*c*) the relief under TA 1970, s.17 for a daughter's services can be claimed in respect of a son or a daughter;

(*d*) the full relief for blind persons under TA 1970, s.18 may be claimed by a person who is a registered blind person for the whole *or part of* the year.

For the levels of relief, see Simon's Tax Intelligence 1978 Finance Act Digest p.4 or Whillans's Tax Tables 1978-79, pp.20 and 21.

Rates of Income Tax
FA 1978, ss.13, 14

For full details see Simon's Tax Intelligence 1978 Finance Act Digest, p.5 or Whillans's Tax Tables 1978-79, p.17.

The 25 per cent. rate applies to—

(*a*) the husband's taxable income (excluding his wife's relevant earned income) up to £750, and

(*b*) a wife's *relevant earned income only* (after wife's earned income relief) up to £750.

Relevant earned income is a wife's earned income less wife's earned income relief.

Repayments to wives

FA 1978, s.22

After 31 July 1978, any repayment of PAYE tax which has been deducted from a wife's income will be made to her, except where the husband is liable to higher rate tax or where the wife has earned income other than Schedule E, for example, under Schedule D as a trader.

The tax repayment attributable to the wife is computed after allowing relief due to her for retirement annuity payments and surplus reliefs not absorbed by the husband due to an insufficiency of income. In no case is the total repayment to exceed the tax deducted under PAYE from the wife's earnings during the year.

The inspector will notify both the husband and the wife of the amount of the repayment due. Any appeal must be made to the General Commissioners except where neither spouse is resident in the United Kingdom, when the appeal is to the Special Commissioners.

The Board are empowered to make regulations by statutory instrument modifying these provisions and for the first such instrument see the Income Tax (Repayments to wives) Regulations 1978, No. 1117 reproduced in Simon's Tax Intelligence, 25 August 1978, pp.430-432.

Retirement annuities

FA 1978, s.26

A person with a retirement annuity contract with a life office can transfer the value of his accrued benefits to another office on better terms. This is commonly known as the "open market" option. The same facility is given to a person's widow, widowers or other dependant.

Power is given for the Board of Inland Revenue to approve

annuity contracts which provide for a payment in respect of a person's accrued rights thereunder to another life office as the premium for an annuity contract with that office.

If the annuity payable under the original contract would have been treated as earned income of the annuitant, then any annuity payable under the substituted contract will be similarly treated. See Simon's Tax Intelligence, 22 December 1978, p.570.

Schedule D, Case III
Dunmore v. McGowan C.A. [1978] S.T.C. 217

Bank interest is received when credited to the account.

Schedule D, Case V
Simon's Tax Intelligence, 4 August 1978, p.362

Deficiencies of income from lettings of overseas property may in practice be carried forward for set-off against future income from the same property (but not against income from any other Case V source). This new practice will be applied by the Inland Revenue to all claims unsettled at 29 July 1977 and to claims made thereafter.

Stamp duty

Conveyance in consideration of a debt. Stamp duty on a transfer of property at arm's length is chargeable by reference to the price paid. Where the price is the discharge of an existing debt owing to the transferee, stamp duty is accordingly chargeable by reference to the amount of indebtedness agreed to be discharged even if that amount was greater than the value of the property transferred. (See SP 5/78 reproduced in Simon's Tax Intelligence, 17 November 1978, p.534.)

Relief from stamp duty on amalgamations. Relief from stamp duty on an amalgamation by way of share exchange or the transfer of shares to an unlimited company, can be obtained under FA 1927, s.55 as amended by FA 1930, s.41 because it is not necessary for the particular existing company to be a limited liability company, Chelsea Land & Investment Ltd. v. I.R. Coms. C.A. [1978] S.T.C. 221.

Forward Notes

Capital Gains Tax
The legislation is to be consolidated during 1979.

Directors' remuneration
The Inland Revenue is to take steps to speed up the collection of tax due on directors' remuneration by improving liaison between accounts and PAYE sections, training staff, concentrating the work in larger specialised offices, giving wider powers to collectors to fix a company's tax bill, charging interest on arrears of directors' PAYE tax and clearing up uncertainty on bonuses and fees.

Life assurance premiums
FA 1976, Sch.4, further amended by FA 1978, s.25 and Sch.3, introduces from 6 April 1979 a new system (premium relief by deduction) of allowing tax relief on life assurance premiums.

Petroleum Revenue Tax
In a statement to the House of Commons on 2 August 1978 a number of proposed changes to PRT were announced, designed to increase the share in profits from North Sea oil and gas taken by the government.

Subject	*Note of further developments*

The changes are—

(*a*) to increase the rate of PRT from 45 per cent. to 60 per cent. from 1 January 1979;

(*b*) to reduce the "uplift" given for certain capital expenditure from 75 per cent. to 35 per cent. for qualifying expenditures under contracts made after 2 August 1978;

(*c*) to reduce from 1 January 1979 the "oil allowance" from 1 million long tons a year to ½ million metric tonnes a year.

(For the full text of the statement, see Simon's Tax Intelligence, 11 August 1978, pp.367-371.)

Schedule D, Cases I and II
Current year basis of assessment. The Inland Revenue has announced first thoughts on the abolition of the preceding year basis of assessment, see the Press Release, 9 October 1978, reproduced in Simon's Tax Intelligence, 20 October 1978, p.480.

Stock relief
A consultative paper explaining how proposals for writing-off part of the stock relief given for earlier years and to limit the build-up of potential liability for future years has been produced by the Inland Revenue, see Simon's Tax Intelligence, 12 January 1979,

Subject	*Note of further developments*

p.585. Broadly the proposal is that the "Schedule 10 relief" will be written off in 1979. Relief under FA 1976 will be written off after six years. Previous reliefs and clawbacks will be dealt with on a "first in first out" basis. Legislation is likely to be included in FA 1979.

Traded options
Whether CGT "wasting asset rules" are properly attributable to traded options (with a chargeable gain arising even when, before brokerage charges, a real loss is made) is a likely subject for FA 1979.